Collins

Cherry Blossoms

Art and Craft

UKG

FS3

SERIES EDITOR: RANI THIPPAVAZZULA

Student + Teacher			Teacher-only	
a animations	**ia** activities	**g** games	**lp** lesson plans	**tn** teacher's notes
ilt instructor-led tutorials	**w** worksheets	**v** videos	**w** worksheets	**ak** answer keys
	audio			

Preface

Cherry Blossoms provides graded, age-appropriate learning opportunities targeting holistic skill development for children in the age group of 3 years to 8 years. The series aligns with the vision outlined in the National Education Policy, 2020 for early years. It spreads across five levels, Nursery (Foundational Stage 1) to Class 2 (Foundational Stage 5). The books use a combination of hands-on activities, frequent recapitulation and child-friendly artwork to facilitate learning.

The series comprises **40 books** and spans **English**, **Maths**, **General Awareness**, and **Art and Craft**. The series comes bundled with a **workbook** for each subject and a book of **rhymes** and **stories** for Foundational Stage 1 to 3.

This series integrates the essence of **NIPUN Bharat** guidelines, which extensively deal with Foundational Literacy and Numeracy. The series aims to motivate learners to read independently, to improve their vocabulary, number sense and spatial understanding. The **Foundational Literacy and Numeracy (FLN)** skills include the skills for developing their critical thinking, logical reasoning and creative skills, as well as the skills to enhance their ability to express themselves both verbally and in writing.

Cherry Blossoms Teacher Support Materials include:

Teacher's Resource Books: Comprises stories, activity banks, classroom management and assessment guidelines

Multimedia eBook: Consists of animations, audio, video, slide shows, and interactive exercises

Print-ready Worksheets: Additional worksheets for practice and reinforcement, present in the digital support

Digital Flashcards: Flashcards with embedded sounds and animations for letter formation and letter-sound association

Animations and Songs: Animated stories and rhymes set to tune

Interactive Games: Interactivities to reinforce concepts in a fun and engaging manner

A note on the activity banks (included in the Teacher's Manuals)

The activity banks comprise hands-on activities that will help children develop the requisite skills to attain age-appropriate learning goals. In keeping with Howard Gardener's theory of multiple intelligences, the activity banks include options and variations that enable teachers to provide a planned cycle of experiences and opportunities, which foster each type of intelligence, to every child in their classrooms. The activity banks equip teachers to use the strengths of children as a means of complementing their less developed areas by valuing and nurturing the inherent abilities of the children.

Rani Thippavazzula, former Academic Director, Ravindra Bharathi Group is an eminent educationist with over two decades of experience in teaching, administration and curriculum design and development. As an Academic Advisor for chain schools pan India, she is proficient in developing learning products and is a specialist in Differentiated Instruction, Enterprise Education and Early Childhood Education.

Learning and Development During the Early Years

The early years are the most significant years for growth, development and learning. During this period, children need adequate opportunities for stimulating experiences as these favourably affect various learning abilities. Learning experiences, when chosen and planned properly, fuel the innate curiosity of children, and stimulate their thought processes.

The goal of learning during the early years is to enhance the all-round development of personality and to inculcate healthy attitudes, life skills and good values. Creative play, well thought-out games and developmentally appropriate activities help children develop the necessary skills to achieve these goals. The skills that children need to acquire can broadly be categorized as:

Motor:
Motor skills pertain not only to gross motor activities like walking and jumping but also include fine motor activities like the ability to hold a pencil and write. The development of motor skills is facilitated through several graded activities.

Personal, Social and Emotional:
Personal, social and emotional development, necessary for the overall personality development of children, is achieved using a combination of hands-on activities, role plays and thought-provoking stories and rhymes.

Linguistic:
The ability to listen, speak, read and write is critical to success in formal learning environments.

Mathematical:
The development of mathematical ideas and concepts is important at this stage since children will continue to build on this learning for most of their years of schooling.

Knowledge and Understanding of the World:
This is achieved through activities that enable children to explore their surroundings at home and in the school, and interact with the people that they see around them.

Health and Safety: The idea of health and safety is introduced through activities, stories and retelling of real-life experiences to encourage children to focus on health and well-being.

Creative:
Creative skills are developed through a host of activities involving art, craft, painting, roleplays, etc.

Logical and Rational Thinking:
Activities that involve simple puzzles, pattern-completion and visual discrimination help children to develop logical and rational thinking skills.

Contents

WALKTHROUGH

A variety of tracing and colouring activities to further fine motor development in an enjoyable manner

Free-hand drawing and colouring pages to support creative development

Rolling, flattening and shaping modelling clay and cotton to support motor development

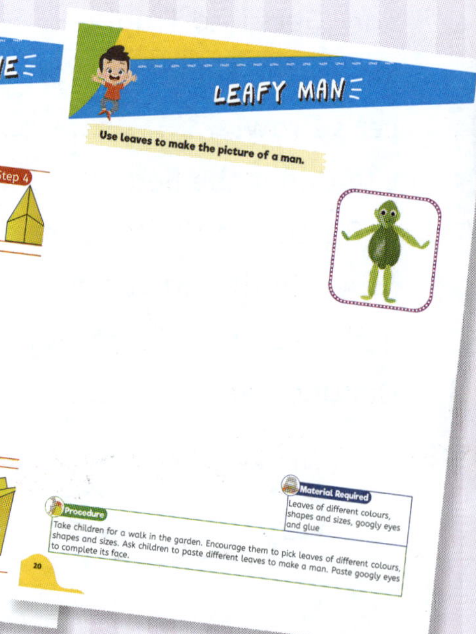

Tearing, pasting, cutting to impove hand-eye coordination and develop the ability to grip objects

Cross-curricular linkages in activities to help support overall learning development

LITTLE RED RIDING HOOD MAZE

Take Little Red Riding Hood to her granny.

GINGERBREAD MAN SYMMETRY

Colour as shown in the other half.

LET'S DRAW!

Draw and colour anything you like.

ANIMAL JUNCTION

Colour the animals as per the colour code.

Group 1

1 green frog
2 red crabs
1 pink hippo
2 orange cats

Group 2

1 blue crab
1 yellow cat
2 red frogs
1 purple hippo

PICTURE SUDOKU

Draw and colour the missing fruits without repeating any image in a row

STEP-BY-STEP DRAWING

Trace the lines to draw a cat in six easy steps.

Step 1

Step 2

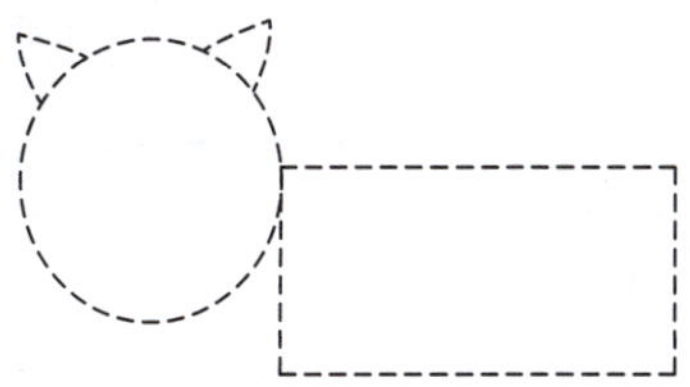

Step 3

Step 4

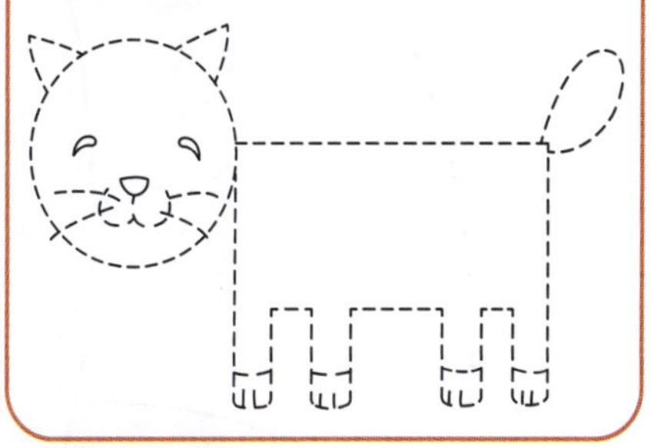

Step 5

Step 6

Draw your cat here.

COLOUR-CODED UMBRELLA

Colour the umbrella as per the colour code.

THREE LITTLE PUPS

Once upon a time, there lived three happy little pups with their mother. The pups grew up big to start their own life. Let us colour the picture and get them ready to start the journey of life.

STRAW HOUSE FOR PUPS

Listen to the story. Help the first pup to build the house.

Material Required
A fresh leaf and green poster colour

Procedure Put green poster colour on a fresh leaf and print the impression to complete the first pup's house.

STICK HOUSE FOR PUPS

Listen to the story. Use ice-cream sticks to make the house for the second pup. Use pencil colours to colour the words that end with 'ut'.

hut rat but sit nut

cut pot

net bib

Material Required

Ice-cream sticks, glue and child-safe scissors

BRICK HOUSE FOR PUPS

Listen to the story. Help the third pup to build the house.

How many bricks did th pup use?

____

Procedure

Cut brown paper into a triangular shape. Paste it to make the roof. Paste squares of red paper to make the bricks. Ask children to count the number of bricks they have pasted.

Material Required

Red origami paper cut into 1 in. sq., brown origami paper, child-safe scissors and glue

PAPER PLATE WOLF

Listen to the story. Make the wolf with a paper plate to bring him back to his home.

Material Required

1 small paper plate, black and red origami paper, child-safe scissors and glue

Procedure

Tear black origami paper into pieces and paste it on the paper plate to make the wolf. Take red origami paper and cut it in oval shape to make the nose of the wolf. Paste red origami paper, cut into a triangle, to make the ears. Paste googly eyes to complete the wolf.

LEAFY MAN

Use leaves to make the picture of a man.

Material Required

Leaves of different colours, shapes and sizes, googly eyes and glue

Procedure

Take children for a walk in the garden. Encourage them to pick leaves of different colours, shapes and sizes. Ask children to paste different leaves to make a man. Paste googly eyes to complete its face.

SIGHT WORDS CODE

Read the words. Colour as per the word.

DAYS OF THE WEEK

Paste colourful origami paper to show the days of the week. Follow the colour code below.

Material Required

Origami paper in different colours, child-safe scissors and glue

Procedure

Cut the sheets of the origami paper as per the colour code. Paste them in the correct sequence to show the days of the week.

SIGHT WORDS CODE

Read the words. Colour as per the word.

ORIGAMI AIRPLANE

Make your own airplane with paper folding.

Step 1

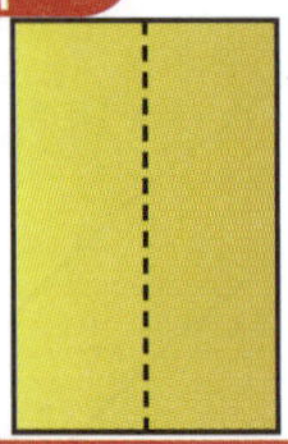

Step 2

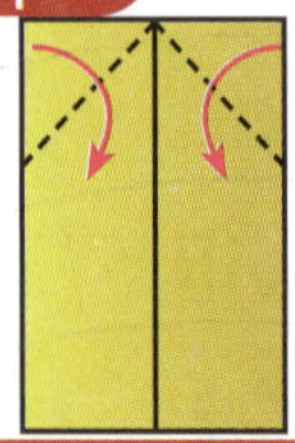

Step 3

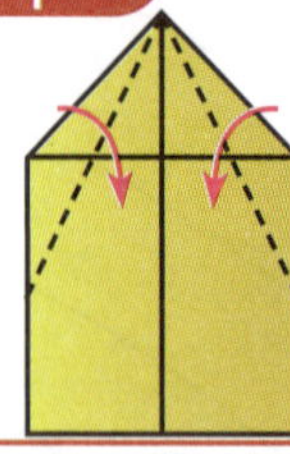

Step 4

Step 5

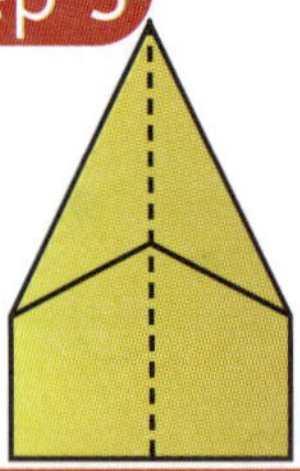

Step 6

Step 7

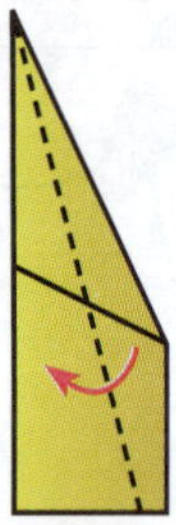

Step 8

Paste here

Step 9

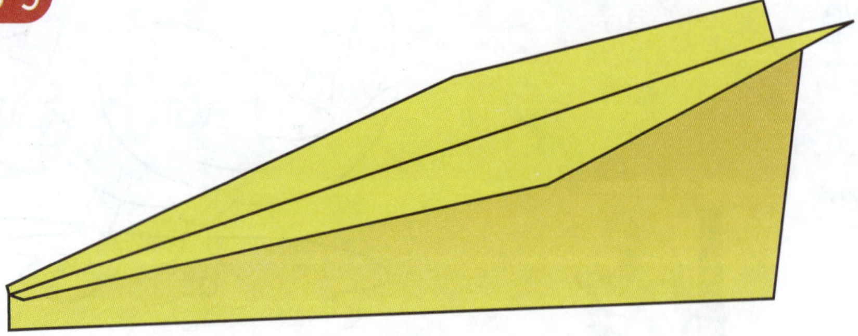

GRID POLAR BEAR

Trace the polar bear in the second grid. Colour both the pictures.

MY SAILBOAT

Use ice-cream sticks to make the sailboat.

Material Required

Ice-cream sticks, brown poster colour, paintbrush, white paper (cut in triangular shape), blue paper and glue

Procedure

Paint ice-cream sticks brown to make the boat. Paste one ice-cream stick vertically and use white paper to make the sail of the boat. Colour the sea using blue crayon. Tear and paste blue paper around the boat to show waves.

SAM GETS INTO TROUBLE

Sam loves sports, but sometimes it gets him into trouble. Look at the pictures. Number these pictures from 1-4 to describe what could have happened.

MR. TRAFFIC SIGNAL AT WORK

Colour the picture as per the colour code.

LET'S DRAW!

Draw and colour anything you like.

LIFE UNDER THE SEA

Help the dolphin find her family.

REFLECTION IN THE ICY LAKE

Trace and colour the picture to make the reflection in water.

ALIENS IN THE ATTIC

Circle the picture that comes next.

LET'S CELEBRATE EARTH DAY

Colour the happy earth in blue and green. Colour the sad earth in black to show pollution around it.

Material Required

Blue and green crayons, black poster colour, paintbrush and glue

Procedure

Tell children the benefits of green earth. Colour the happy earth in blue and green. Colour the sad earth. Paint the cotton black and paste it on the outer circle of the sad earth to show pollution. Children can also use black crayon to give the highlights the effects of pollution for sad earth.

BUZZING BEE

Make yarn-wrapped buzzing bees.

Material Required

Cardboard, yellow poster colour, black origami paper, long lengths of black yarn, googly eyes, child-safe scissors, black sketch pen and glue

Procedure

Cut the cardboard in the shape of the bee. Make 4 small triangular snips on the body of the bee. Paint the cardboard yellow. Cut out the antennae and the tail of the bee from the black origami paper. Wrap the yarn through the snips to make the black stripes. Paste the antennae, tail and eyes. Draw the mouth of the bee to complete it.

LET'S DRAW!

Draw and colour anything you like.

BIRD IN A NEST

Make a bird and its nest using origami paper and feathers.

Material Required

1 small paper plate, brown, yellow and red origami paper, black sketch pen, child-safe scissors, feathers and glue

Procedure

Cut out the shape of the bird from red origami paper and paste it on the paper plate. Paste small cut pieces of brown origami on the bottom half of the paper plate to show the nest. Paste yellow origami paper (cut in a triangular shape) to make the beak. Use black sketch pen to make the eye of the bird and paste feathers on the tail to complete the bird.

PATTERN DOODLES

Using crayons, make any patterns you like on the balloons.

BEACH BALL

Finger paint to make a beach ball.

Procedure

Invert the paper plate on the page. Using a black sketch pen, divide the plate into sections as shown. Dip a finger in poster colour and print to complete the section of the ball. Use a different colour for each section.

Material Required

Paper plate, poster colours of different colours, black sketch pen and glue

PICTURE SUDOKU

Draw and colour the missing pictures to complete the pattern.

GEOMETRIC ROBOT

Let's make a robot with different shapes.

Procedure

Cut differently coloured foam sheets into different shapes. Paste the shapes to make the robot. Use black sketch pen to make the eyes.

Material Required

Foam sheets of different colours, child-safe scissors, black sketch pen and glue

SNOWMAN TO LIFE

Decorate the snowman as shown in the given image. Use brown wool to make his hands.

Procedure

Apply white poster colour on a toothbrush and spray it with your thumb to make snowfall on the page. Use white cotton/ cotton balls to make the snowman. Paste brown wool to make its hands and decorate the snowman as you like.

Material Required

1 toothbrush, white poster colour, cotton, decorative material and glue

THANK YOU CARD

Make a thank you card. Write the names of the people on the card whom you would like to thank. Paste the card on the page.

FAIRY PRINCESS CASTLE

Use your hand to make a castle for the fairy princess.

Procedure

Dip a hand in a poster colour and print it on the page. When the paint dries, use different sketch pens to make windows, doors and flags to complete the castle.

Material Required

Poster colour and sketch pens in different colours

SUMMER TIME AT THE BEACH

Dip ear buds in paint and use them to make the beach scene.

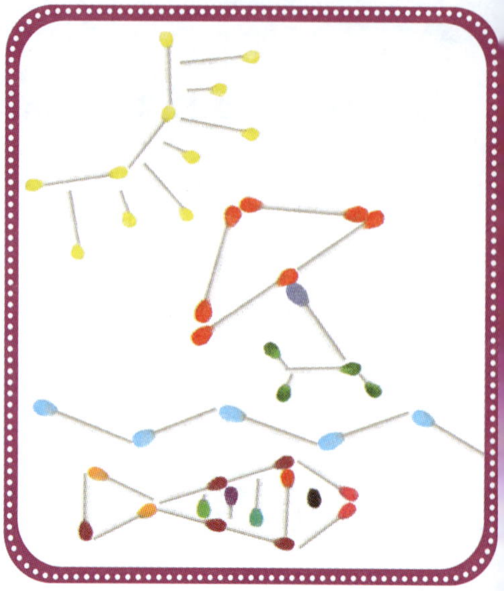

HAPPY YELLOW DUCK

Use crushed crepe paper to make the duck.

MY MAGIC CARPET

Make your own magic carpet here.

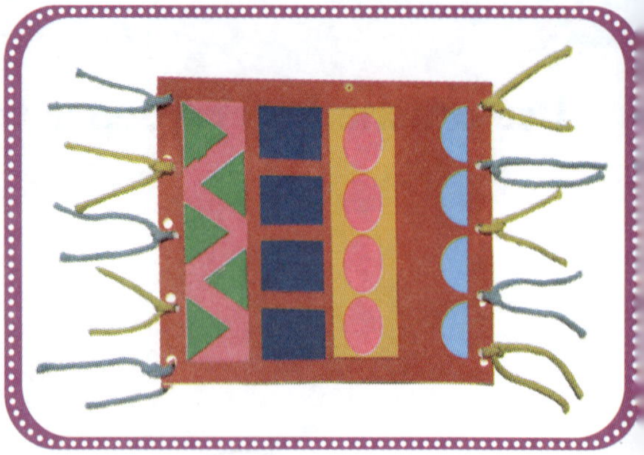

Material Required

Wool, coloured origami paper, child-safe scissors and glue.

Procedure

Cut coloured origami paper into different shapes and paste it on the carpet to make a pattern. Paste short lengths of wool along the two short edges of the carpet to complete it.

LET'S DRAW!

Draw and colour anything you like.

OLYMPIC RINGS

Make Olympic rings with paper cups and poster colours.

LET'S COLOUR

Colour the picture to complete it.

OPP-POP GOES THE POPCORN

Match the opposite popcorns. Use ice-cream sticks to make the popcorn boxes.

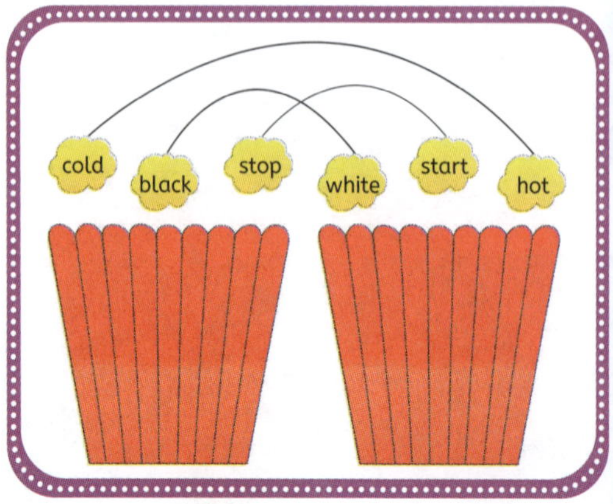

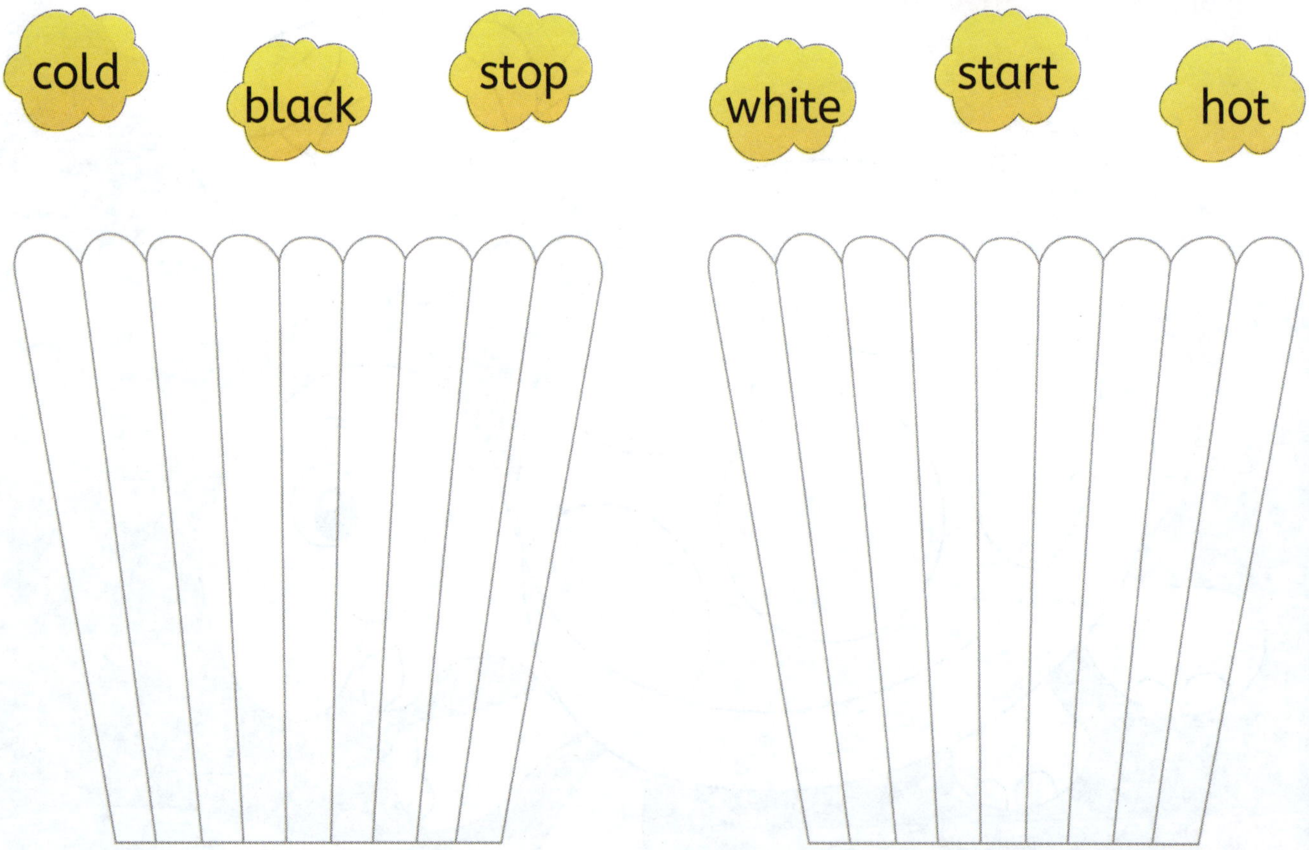

Procedure

Once children match the opposites, they can paint the ice-cream sticks in any colour they want and make the popcorn boxes.

Material Required

Ice-cream sticks, glue and poster colours

STORY TIME

Listen to the story. Draw and colour the alligator family.

LET'S WALK THE JUNGLE

Colour and print to complete the jungle scene.

Teacher's Note

Involve children in group discussion where they discuss the names of the animals. Once they are familiar, ask them to thumbprint the big animals and colour the small animals.

STEP-BY-STEP DRAWING

Trace the lines to draw a butterfly in eight easy steps.

Step 1

Step 2

Step 3

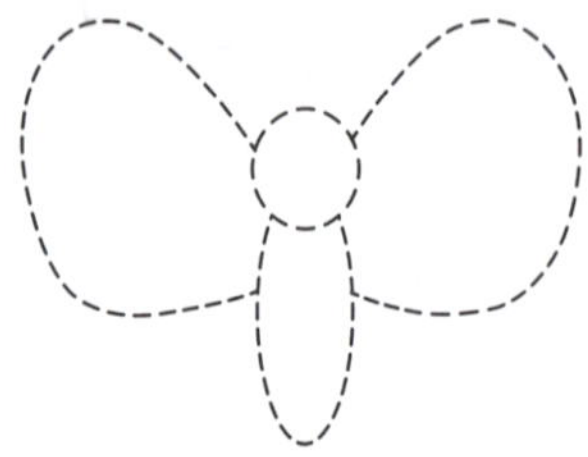

Draw your butterfly here

Step 4

Step 5

Step 6

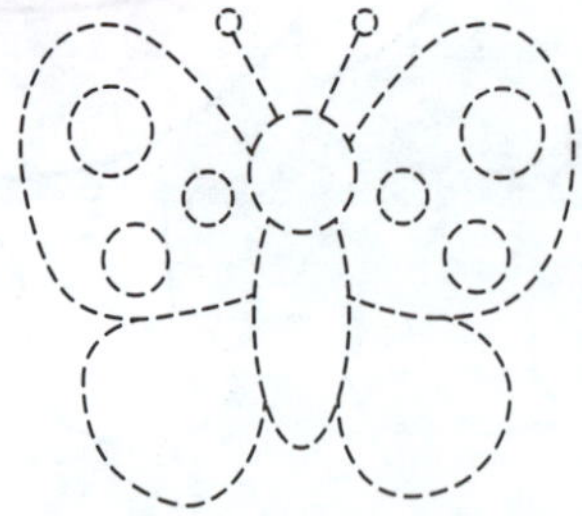

Step 7

Step 8

ORIGAMI BOAT

Make your own boat with paper folding.

Step 1

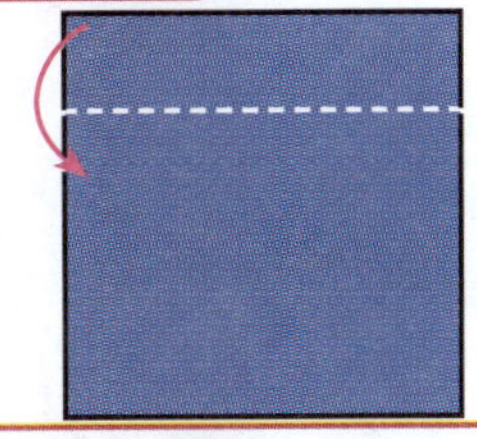

Step 2

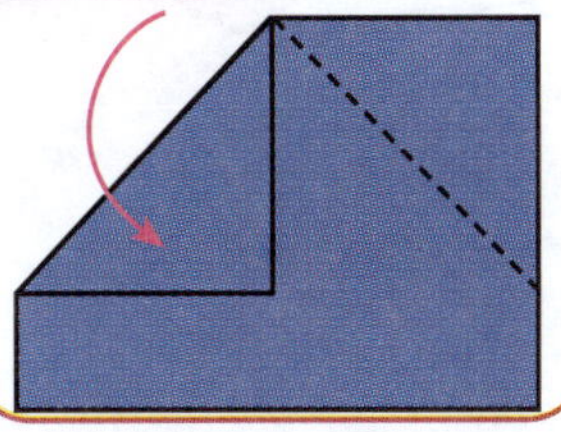

Step 3

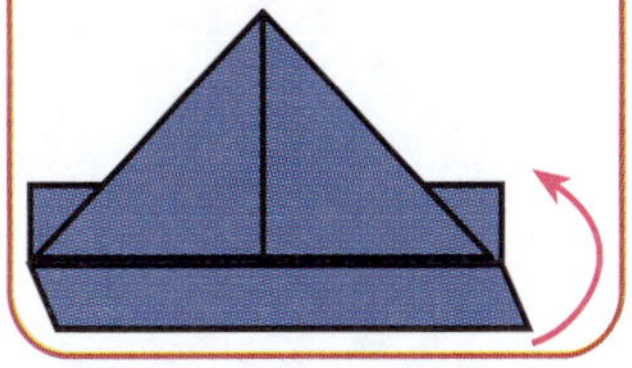

Step 4

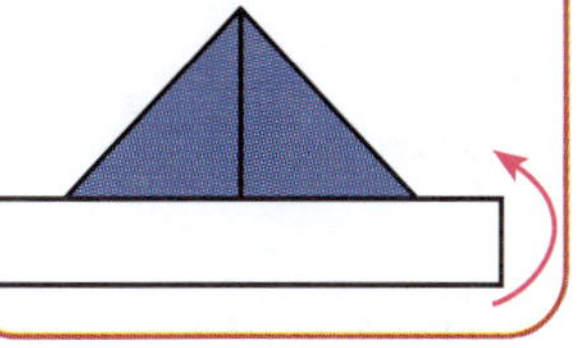

Step 5

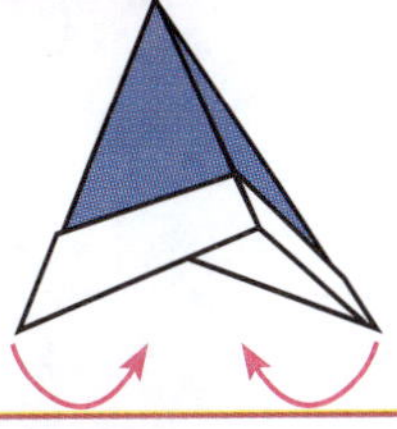

Step 6

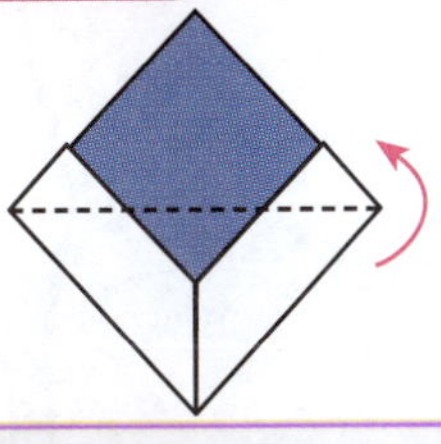

Step 7

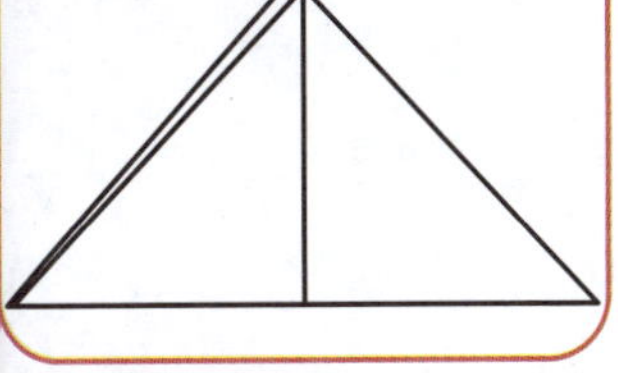

Step 8

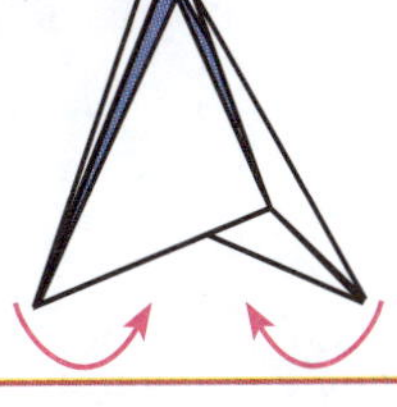

Paste here

Step 9

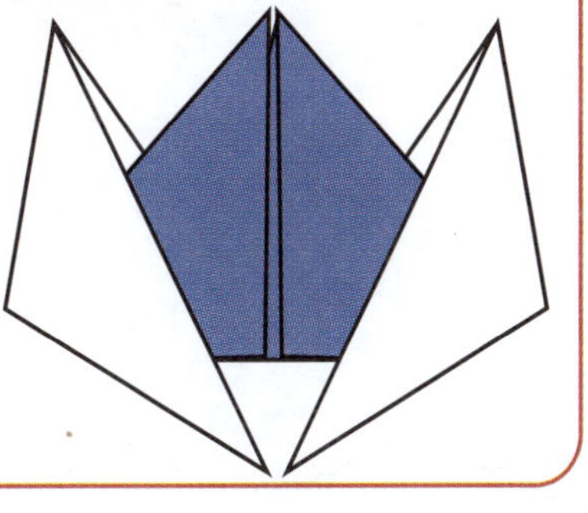

Step 10

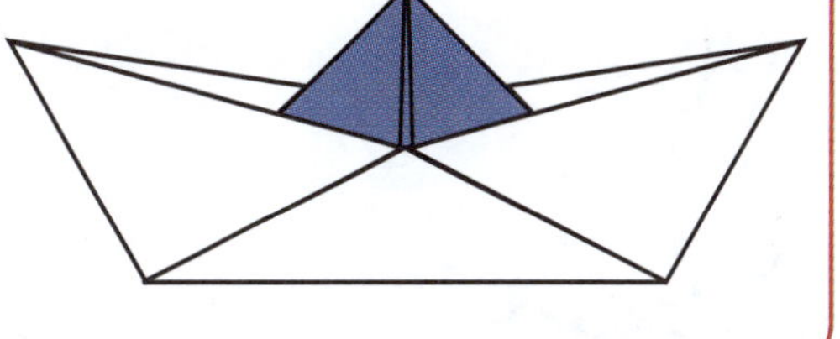

LET'S DRAW!

Draw and colour anything you like.

PATTERN SUDOKU

Complete the grid by drawing the missing image. Colour the image.

MY FIRST WATERCOLOUR PAINTING

Use poster colours and a paintbrush to paint any picture you like.

LET'S DRAW!

Draw and colour anything you like.

ORIGAMI CAR

Make your own car with paper folding.

Step 1

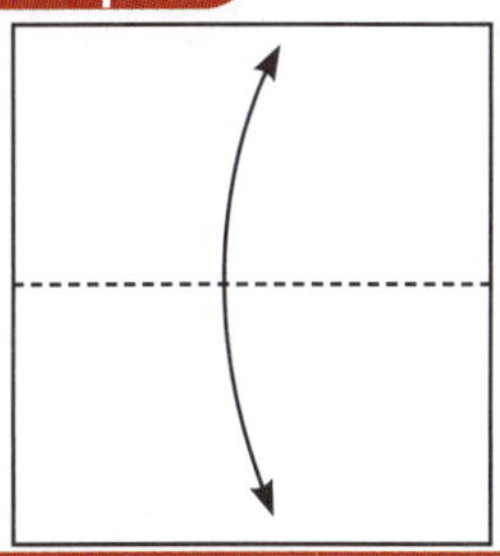

Step 2

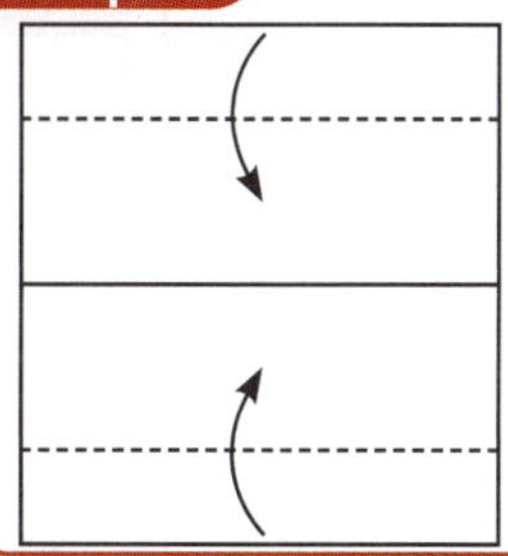

Step 3

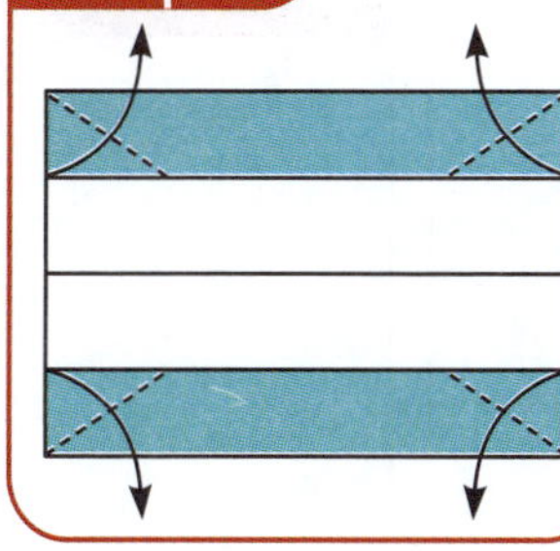

Step 4

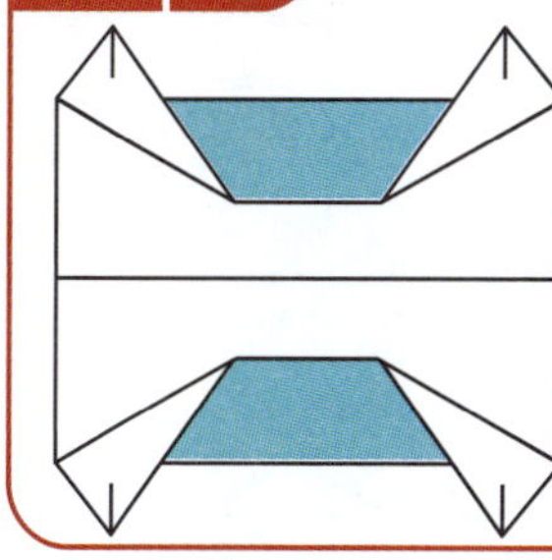

Step 5

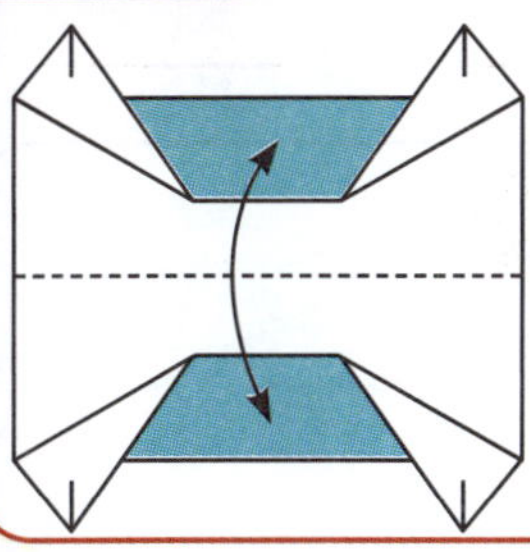

Paste here

Step 6

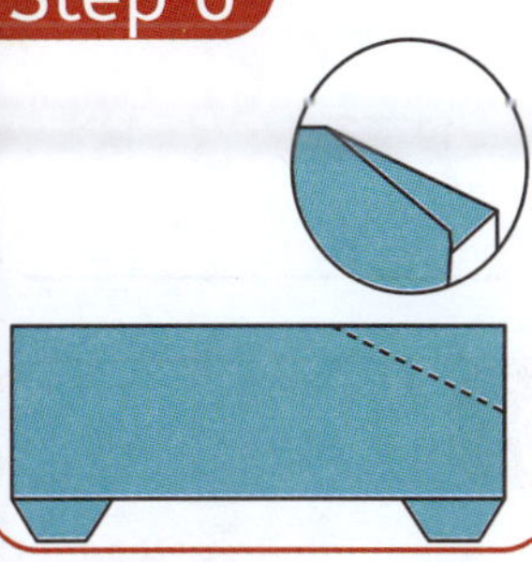

Step 7

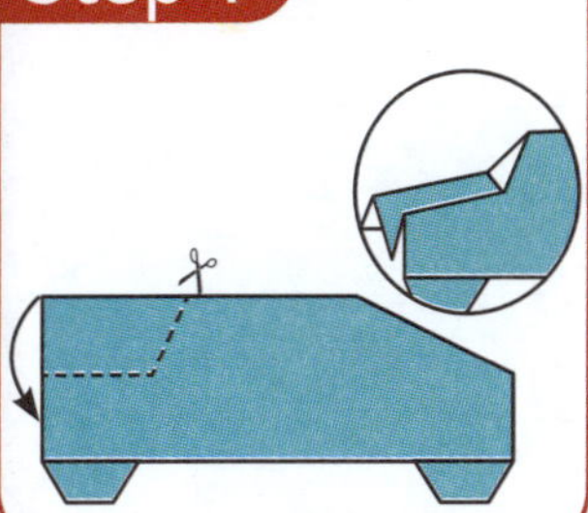

Step 8

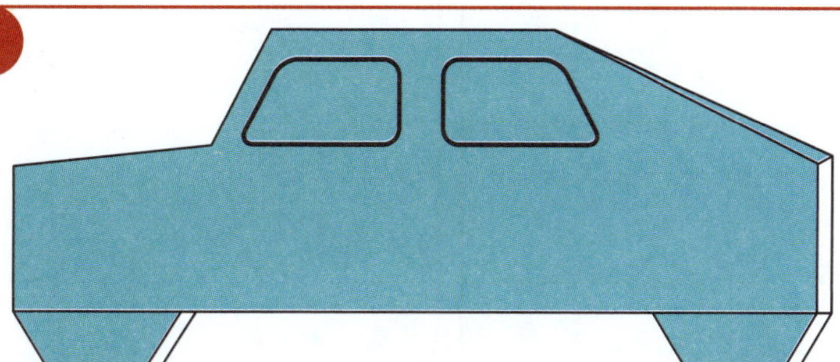

STEP-BY-STEP DRAWING

Trace the lines and learn to draw a car in 12 easy steps.

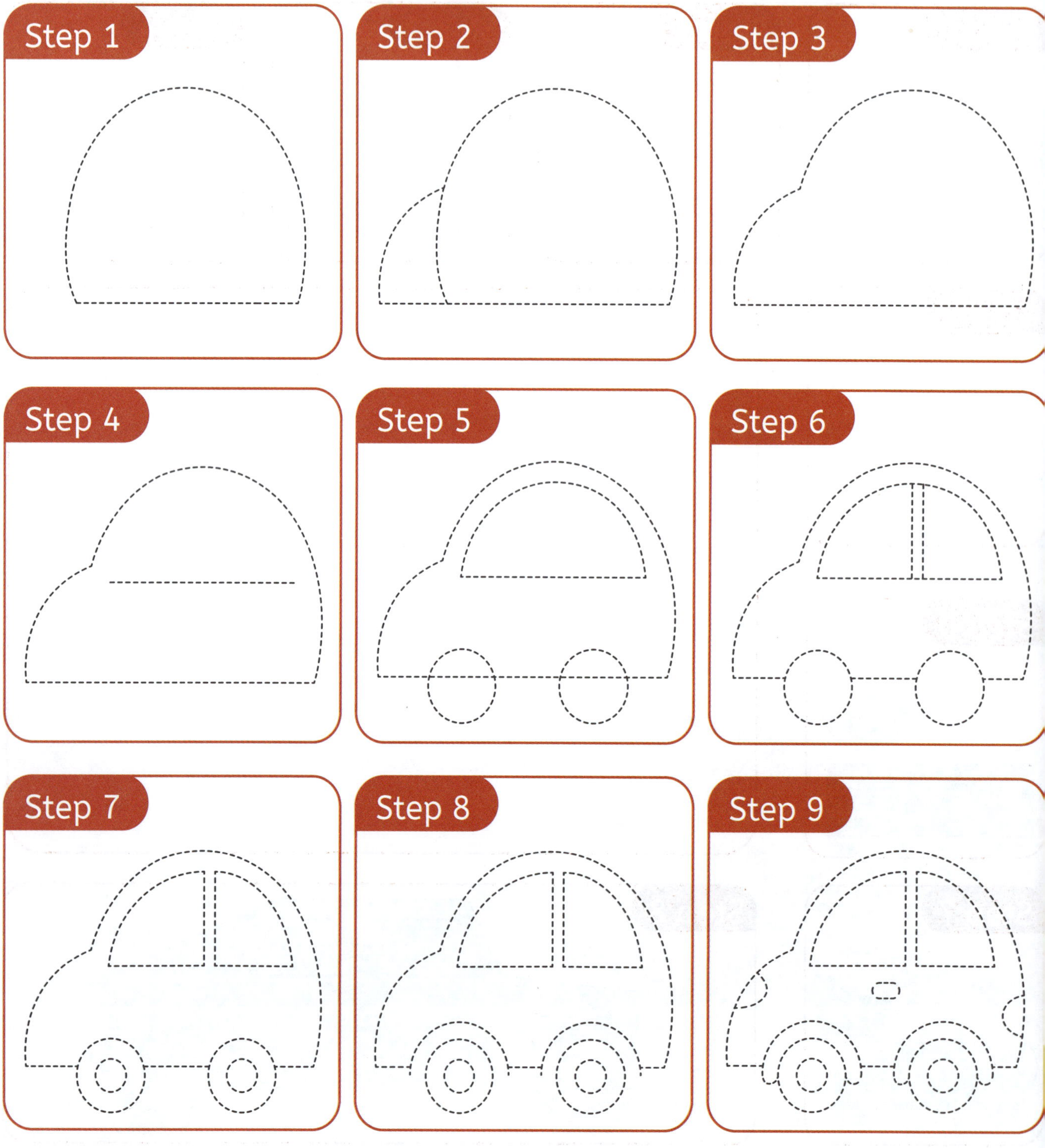

Step 10

Step 11

Step 12

Draw your car here.

LET'S DRAW!

Draw and colour anything you like.